JPR WILLIAMS

The Rugby Legend's Autobiography

Richard M. Jackson

TABLE OF CONTENTS

INTRODUCTION

CHAPTER 1 Who is JPR Williams

    1.1: Formative Years

CHAPTER 2:Passion for Rugby

    2.1: Introduction to Pro Rugby

CHAPTER 3: Special Games

    3.1: Wins

CHAPTER 4:Team Dynamics

    4.1: Companionship

CHAPTER 5: Difficulties

    5.1:Setbacks

CHAPTER 6: Leadership in fields

    6.1: Off-field Leadership

CHAPTER 7: Personal Reflection

    7.1:Life Beyond Rugby

CHAPTER 8:Legacy on the Sport

    8.1:Impact on the Sport

CONCLUSION

INTRODUCTION

John Peter Rhys Williams, also known as JPR Williams, is a former Welsh rugby union player who made a lasting impression on the game. Williams, who was born in Bridgend, Wales, on March 2, 1949, became well-known for being a daring and stubborn fullback. Throughout his remarkable career, which lasted from the late 1960s to the early 1980s, he played a significant role for both the British and Irish Lions and the Welsh national side. Acknowledged as one of the most memorable personalities in rugby history, JPR Williams is recognized for his remarkable abilities, tough style of play, and unusual facial hair.

When JPR Williams represented Wales in international competition in 1969, he built a name for himself as a dependable and aggressive player. Known for his outstanding defensive skills, he was instrumental in helping Wales win the Five Nations Championship in 1971, 1976, and 1978, achieving a Grand Slam.

Williams was a vital member of the British and Irish Lions during their historic series victory against New Zealand in 1971, in addition to his success with the Welsh national squad. He became a fan favorite due to his everlasting dedication and determined efforts on the field.

Williams was well-known for his academic accomplishments in addition to his rugby skills. He followed a profession in medicine, qualifying as a surgeon while succeeding in the competitive world of international rugby at the same time.

JPR Williams developed a reputation as one of the sport's hardest-working and most dedicated athletes during his playing career. He became a rugby legend because of his reckless style and unusual beard, which became his signature. He remained an influential figure in rugby after quitting the professional game, teaching, and commentating on it.

CHAPTER 1 Who Is JPR Williams

Former Welsh rugby union player JPR Williams In the 1970s, he was a fullback for both the British and Irish Lions and Wales. Williams is renowned for his extraordinary abilities and career-long contributions to rugby.

Born in Bridgend, Wales, on March 2, 1949, Jonathan Peter Rhys Williams, also referred to as JPR Williams, was raised. As a rugby player, he rose to fame and became one of the game's most recognizable characters.

JPR Williams was a fullback who was renowned for his aggressive and daring style of play. In the 1970s, he was a vital member of the British and Irish Lions and the Welsh national team. He was notably a member of the Welsh side that won the Five Nations Championship (now known as the Six Nations) in 1971, 1976, and 1978, achieving a Grand Slam.

Additionally impressive were his efforts on the British and Irish Lions tours. JPR Williams was a member of the renowned 1971 Lions journey to New Zealand, during which the team won an unprecedented series.

JPR Williams pursued a career in medicine off the field and became a licensed surgeon. Even after quitting rugby, he stayed active in the game and kept up his development contributions. One of the greatest players in Welsh and British rugby history is JPR Williams.

1.1: Formative Years

JPR Williams, a former Welsh rugby union player best remembered for his outstanding fullback career, was born John Peter Rhys Williams on March 2, 1949. He did well academically and athletically in his early years, especially rugby. Williams made his Wales debut in 1969 and quickly established himself as a formidable runner and defensive specialist. His contributions to the Welsh team's victories in 1971, 1976, and 1978 were vital in their success during the 1970s.

JPR Williams went to Bridgend Grammar School before enrolling at St. Thomas' Hospital Medical School in London to pursue his medical studies. He pursued a successful medical career as an orthopedic surgeon despite his devotion to rugby.

Williams rose to fame on the rugby pitch for his daring style of play, frequently making big tackles and kicking with remarkable accuracy. He was a pivotal player in

Welsh rugby in the 1970s because of his exceptional athleticism and commitment to the game.

Williams was a successful member of the Welsh national team in addition to playing for the British and Irish Lions on two tours (1971 and 1974). In the rugby community, his on-field impact and unique playing style have left a lasting legacy.

CHAPTER 2:Passion for Rugby

The renowned Welsh rugby player JPR Williams had an unrivaled love for the game. His bold playing style demonstrated his commitment to rugby, cementing his place among the game's all-time great fullbacks. Williams' passion for rugby was evident in his contributions to the sport long after he retired, demonstrating that his love for the game went beyond the field.

Rugby player JPR Williams demonstrated an unwavering dedication to the game, as evidenced by his legendary performances with the British and Irish Lions. His passion extended beyond personal success, inspiring a sense of camaraderie among teammates that has endured throughout the rugby community. Many were inspired by Williams' unwavering love of rugby, which helped to establish his status as a genuine representative of the game's best players.

2.1: Introduction to Pro Rugby

The legendary Welsh rugby player JPR Williams started playing professionally in the late 1960s. He debuted for Wales in 1969 and is well-known for his bold and energetic style. Williams played fullback most of his career and was a member of the Welsh side that won Grand Slams in 1971, 1976, and 1978.

On the field, his unique look—a red scrum cap and a mustache—made him instantly identifiable. Beyond his accomplishments on the international front, Williams' extraordinary abilities and dedication to the game were crucial to the British and Irish Lions' tour triumph.

One of the greatest rugby players of all time, JPR Williams is renowned for his strong presence, defensive prowess, and significant contribution to Wales' rugby history.

JPR Williams began his rugby career with the Neath RFC in 1967. He was born John Peter Rhys Williams on March 2, 1949, in Bridgend, Wales. Williams rose to prominence rapidly thanks to his exceptional kicking ability, fearless tackling style, and powerful sprinting. In

1969, he made his Wales debut internationally against England.

Williams played a key role in the Welsh team's dominance in the early 1970s Five Nations Championship. His combative spirit and athleticism were on full display not just in his Wales exploits but also on the British and Irish Lions tours, where he was instrumental in the team's 1971 series victory over New Zealand.

Williams achieved success in rugby as well as medicine, going on to become a licensed surgeon. Even though he had several injuries during his playing career, he nevertheless made a big impact on Welsh rugby up to his retirement in 1981. JPR Williams continued to be active in rugby after retiring, contributing his observations as a pundit.

His influence on the game, both on and off the field, cemented JPR Williams' reputation as one of the greatest rugby players in Welsh history.

CHAPTER 3: Special Games

During his career, Welsh rugby hero JPR Williams had several notable contests. Known for his bold and explosive style of play, one memorable occasion occurred during the 1971 British & Irish Lions tour to New Zealand, where Williams was instrumental in the team's victory in the series. His contributions to Wales' Grand Slam win in the Five Nations Championships of 1970 and 1976 are also frequently cited as seminal events in his rugby career.

On the rugby pitch, JPR Williams was a fullback renowned for his extraordinary abilities and daring demeanor. He was instrumental in helping the Lions win the series during their 1971 trip to New Zealand with his strong running and good defensive play. JPR's brilliant performance in the third test of that series, which the Lions won, will always be remembered in particular.

JPR Williams was a key member of Wales' team that helped them win a Grand Slam in the 1970 Five Nations Championship. He stood out for his brave tackling and ability to move from fullback into the offensive line.

In the 1976 Five Nations Championship, JPR Williams was instrumental in Wales's victory for a Grand Slam. In addition to showcasing his rugby skills, his performances cemented his place among the greatest players in Welsh rugby history.

3.1: Wins

During his career, Welsh rugby union player JPR Williams earned several noteworthy successes, including three Grand Slams in the Five Nations Championship with the Wales national side in 1971, 1976, and 1978. He was a pivotal player renowned for his extraordinary fullback abilities.
Throughout the 1960s and 1970s, JPR Williams—full name John Peter Rhys Williams—played fullback for

both the British and Irish Lions and Wales. He became well-known for his aggressive style of play and formidable defensive skills. Apart from the Grand Slam triumphs previously stated, Williams had a part in Wales' Triple Crown victories in 1971, 1976, and 1978. Highlights of his career also include his tours with the British and Irish Lions in 1971 and 1974, when he was crucial to their series victories over South Africa and New Zealand, respectively. Williams, who is renowned for his distinctive sideburns, is regarded as one of the best rugby players of all time.

CHAPTER 4:Team Dynamics

The renowned Welsh rugby player JPR Williams was well-known for his strong emphasis on teamwork. His field leadership placed a strong emphasis on teamwork, communication, and working together to succeed as a group. Williams recognized that teamwork is essential to overcoming obstacles and securing success, therefore he encouraged his teams to feel united and supportive of one another.

Known mostly as a fullback, JPR Williams represented Wales in rugby during the 1970s, a time when Welsh rugby experienced significant success. His team's concentration on discipline, diligence, and a common dedication to greatness defined its dynamics. Williams encouraged his teammates to be resilient and determined on the field with his aggressive play style and fearless demeanor. His leadership went beyond personal abilities, stressing the value of group effort and tactical cooperation. Wales achieved a lot at that time, including Grand Slam wins in the Five Nations Championship, thanks in part to this collaborative ethos.

4.1: Companionship

The renowned Welsh rugby player JPR Williams was well-known for his close bond with teammates both on and off the field. During his playing career, his enthusiasm for the game and sense of camaraderie helped the Welsh rugby team achieve victory.

John Peter Rhys Williams, also known as JPR Williams, was a fullback for the British and Irish Lions and Wales in the 1970s. Recognized for his audacious style of play, he played a pivotal role in Wales' success, contributing to their Three-peat wins in the Five Nations Championship in 1971, 1976, and 1978.

Apart from his remarkable abilities in rugby, Williams was acknowledged for cultivating a robust sense of unity among his teammates. The cohesive and encouraging atmosphere was facilitated by his leadership and commitment to the group. Williams' influence went beyond the field, forging enduring bonds with teammates, and his legacy in Welsh rugby lives on in the rich history of the game.

CHAPTER 5: Difficulties

JPR Williams encountered many difficulties during his rugby career. His dedication to playing unwaveringly and fearlessly, frequently risking his life in tackles and aerial duels, was one noteworthy quality. Physical problems were more pronounced during his playing era because rugby players did not have the protection gear that players use today.

Williams also had to deal with the strain of lofty expectations, particularly during Wales' prosperous 1970s campaigns. The Grand Slam wins increased scrutiny and the difficulty of continuing to perform at a high level.

Off the field, juggling his rugby duties and his medical job as a trained surgeon presented another set of difficulties. Notwithstanding these challenges, JPR Williams' tenacity and talent helped him achieve legendary status in the rugby community.

JPR Williams had difficulties both on and off the field throughout his remarkable career. Despite being renowned, his daring style of play put him in danger of physical harm and injury. As a fullback, he frequently found himself in the middle of hard hits and stressful circumstances.

Off the field, juggling his medical job and rugby career brought its own set of difficulties. JPR Williams sought a profession in surgery and was able to juggle the grueling demands of medicine and rugby. The effort needed to play professional rugby on top of his surgical duties demonstrated his versatility and capacity to succeed in many other professions.

Williams's ability to bounce back from these setbacks further cemented his standing as a determined and successful person in the rugby and medical communities.

5.1:Setbacks

During his career, JPR Williams, a former rugby player from Wales, experienced difficulties, including injuries that limited his playing time. Despite these difficulties, he is still regarded as a famous player in rugby history because of his outstanding fullback abilities and his services to the Welsh national team in the 1970s.

Despite having a great rugby career, JPR Williams did have injuries that limited his playing time. One significant setback occurred in 1974 when he suffered a catastrophic knee injury that required extensive recovery time. Williams overcame these obstacles and demonstrated resiliency and willpower by making returns. His reputation as a courageous and brilliant player, together with his overall impact on Welsh rugby, are enduring facets of his legacy.

CHAPTER 6: Leadership in fields

The legendary Welsh rugby player JPR Williams led from the front as a fullback. He set an example with his bold tackles and accurate kicks, and he was well-known for his bravery, skill, and dedication. During his time, his powerful presence made a big difference in the Welsh rugby team's success.

John Peter Rhys Williams, also known as JPR Williams, was a Welsh player from 1969 to 1981. He was a pivotal player in the 1970s Welsh rugby "Golden Era" and was well-known for his daring style of play. Williams was a fullback who was a reliable defender as well as an explosive player who frequently joined the backline with quickness and agility.

His tenacity on the field and his capacity to motivate colleagues demonstrated his leadership abilities. Williams played a key role in the Welsh teams that won the Five Nations Championship in 1971, 1976, and 1978, all of which were Grand Slams. His efforts went above and beyond mere talent, fostering a supportive and harmonious team environment.

Williams demonstrated a well-rounded personality by pursuing a successful medical career off the field. He is regarded as one of the most recognizable personalities in Welsh rugby history and his leadership legacy in the sport endures.

6.1: Off-field Leadership

Legendary Welsh rugby player JPR Williams had great leadership qualities both on and off the field. He was a born leader on the field thanks to his daring and focused style of play, especially when he was a member of the Welsh national team during their prosperous era in the 1970s. Williams remained a well-respected character in rugby off the field and carried on his contributions to the sport through coaching. Beyond the game, he demonstrated his leadership abilities by pursuing a prosperous medical profession and exhibiting self-control and commitment in many areas of his life. JPR Williams was renowned on the field for his remarkable fullback abilities and his unwavering dedication to the game. Throughout the 1970s, he was a key member of the Welsh national team, which helped them win several important tournaments and Grand Slams.

Williams demonstrated leadership on the field by making wise decisions, interacting with teammates, and motivating others with his deeds. His well-known image of himself playing rugby without a headpiece frequently represented his bravery and perseverance on the pitch.

JPR Williams pursued a career in medicine off the field and became a licensed surgeon. His background as a dual professional demonstrated his ability to juggle professional and academic endeavors with elite sports. Beyond his playing career, he remained involved in rugby as a coach and mentor to future players, as well as working as a team doctor.

In conclusion, JPR Williams demonstrated leadership both on and off the field by leading his team to victory and juggling a prosperous medical profession with his involvement in the expansion and advancement of rugby.

CHAPTER 7: Personal Reflection

His dual career as a surgeon and rugby player must have been an interesting and difficult one. It takes extraordinary discipline and time management to juggle the rigors of a medical job with the demands of a professional rugby career.

It's possible that his daring on the rugby pitch reflects a strong love for the game and a willingness to take risks. In particular, choosing to play without a headgear could be a sign of a strong sense of uniqueness and a dedication to authenticity.

Throughout his medical career, JPR Williams probably found satisfaction in improving other people's well-being, demonstrating another facet of his leadership that was based on providing care and assistance to people.

In the end, his personal reflections would be based on his own viewpoint, experiences, and the knowledge he gained from playing rugby and practicing medicine.

his path reveals a diverse and exciting life. As a rugby player, his bold approach and determination to play without headgear would have represented a belief in authenticity and a desire to embrace risks.

In his medical career, Williams certainly experienced difficulty balancing the duties of a surgeon's obligations with the physical demands of professional rugby. His choice to pursue a career in medicine with his rugby responsibilities demonstrates a strong sense of discipline and a desire to make a positive effect beyond the playing arena.

It would be fascinating to study how these experiences affected his perspective on leadership, resilience, and the connection between athletics and medicine. Personal observations from JPR Williams could offer useful insights into the thinking of a dual-professional and a legendary personality in both rugby and the medical industry.

7.1:Life Beyond Rugby

JPR Williams, the Welsh rugby great, sought a career in medicine after retiring from rugby. He became a successful surgeon, specializing in maxillofacial surgery. Williams balanced his medical career with his passion for rugby, leaving a lasting impact both on and off the field.

JPR Williams, born John Peter Rhys Williams on March 2, 1949, not only excelled in rugby but also pursued a notable medical career. After earning his medical degree at St Thomas' Hospital in London, he became a consultant surgeon, focusing on maxillofacial surgery, which deals with injuries to the face and jaw.

Williams played rugby for Wales and the British and Irish Lions during the 1970s, earning a reputation as a fearless and talented fullback. His medical expertise and rugby legacy made him a respected figure in both fields. Williams' contributions to sports and medicine showcase his diverse and impactful life beyond the rugby field.

CHAPTER 8:Legacy on the Sport

JPR Williams, a legendary Welsh rugby player, left a lasting legacy on the sport through his exceptional skills as a fullback. Renowned for his fearless tackling and strong running, he played a key role in Wales' success during the 1970s. Williams' legacy extends beyond his playing days, as he became a respected surgeon, contributing both on and off the field to the world of sports and medicine.

JPR Williams, full name John Peter Rhys Williams, was born on March 2, 1949, in Bridgend, Wales. He gained prominence as a rugby union player during the 1970s, earning 55 caps for the Welsh national team from 1969 to 1981. His remarkable skills as a fullback, characterized by fearless tackling and powerful running, contributed significantly to Wales' success in that era.

Williams was an integral part of the Welsh team that achieved Grand Slam victories in the Five Nations Championship in 1971, 1976, and 1978. He also played a crucial role in the British and Irish Lions tours in 1971 and 1974, notably the series win against the All Blacks in 1971.

Off the field, JPR Williams pursued a career in medicine, becoming a qualified surgeon. This dual expertise in rugby and medicine has added to his legacy, showcasing his intellectual prowess and dedication beyond sports. His impact on the sport endures through the memories of his playing days and the inspiration he provided to future generations of rugby players in Wales and beyond.

8.1:Impact on the Sport

JPR Williams, a legendary Welsh rugby player, had a significant impact on the sport. Renowned for his fearless and dynamic style, he played a key role in Wales' success during the 1970s. Williams, primarily a fullback, was known for his powerful running and strong defensive skills. His contributions helped shape Wales' rugby legacy, and he remains an iconic figure in the history of the sport.

JPR Williams, full name John Peter Rhys Williams, played rugby for Wales from 1969 to 1981, earning 55 caps. His impact was not only due to his athletic abilities but also his influence on the game's culture. Williams was known for his aggressive and fearless playing style, often putting his body on the line for the team.

One of his defining moments came in the 1971 British Lions tour to New Zealand, where he played a crucial role in the Lions' series win. His famous "99 call" defensive strategy, rallying the team to be more aggressive in their tackles, became a lasting legacy.

Off the field, Williams pursued a medical career, becoming a successful surgeon, showcasing the combination of intellect and physical prowess. His lasting impact extends beyond his playing days, as he remains a respected figure in both rugby and the medical community.

CONCLUSION

Thanks to his extraordinary abilities and contributions to the game, the great Welsh rugby player JPR Williams had a lasting impression on the sport. In the 1970s, Williams—who was well-known for his famous sideburns, courageous play, and powerful defensive skills—became an iconic figure in Welsh rugby. He became a rugby icon because of his unwavering dedication to perfection on and off the field. JPR Williams's legacy in rugby will go on since his achievements will inspire upcoming generations of players to pursue greatness in addition to his remarkable athletic abilities.

Welsh rugby union player JPR Williams, whose birth year was 1949, gained notoriety mostly as a fullback. He was dubbed "JPR" and rose to prominence in Welsh rugby in the 1970s as a result of his unwavering commitment and fearlessness on the field.

Williams was a key member of the Wales national squad that won the Five Nations Championship (now known as the Six Nations) three times in a row in 1971, 1976, and 1978, among other spectacular achievements. Outstanding running ability, a fierce work ethic, and excellent defensive abilities all defined his performances.

JPR Williams's famous sideburns, which grew to define his appearance and add to his captivating personality, were one of his distinguishing characteristics. Williams balanced his rugby obligations with his academics by pursuing a profession in medicine off the pitch.

Williams toured with the British and Irish Lions in 1971 and 1974 in addition to his success on the international scene. With Williams playing a pivotal role in the team's victory, the 1971 tour to New Zealand is especially remembered for the Lions' historic series victory over the All Blacks.

As one of the best Welsh rugby players of his time, JPR Williams began his international rugby career in 1981 and went on to leave a lasting legacy. Because he stayed active in the sport and is still seen as a significant character in rugby union history, his influence goes beyond his playing days.

Printed in Dunstable, United Kingdom